All rights reserved. Except as permitted under the U.S. Copyright Act of 1976, no part of this publication may be reproduced, distributed, or transmitted in any form or by any means, or stored in a database or retrieval system, without the prior written permission of the publisher, except for a reviewer, who may quote excerpts from the book for a review. For permission, please direct your written request to the publisher e-mail address provided below:

Pejepublishing@gmail.com

Printed in the United States of America
Copyright© 2015 by Peje-Patrick Malcolm Publishing
ISBN No.: 978-0-9890237-1-9

Interior and Exterior Graphic Design
provided by Irene Michel
illestr8tor@gmail.com

DEDICATION

Thank you for taking a time-out to explore the wonder of PEJETALES©. I am confident you will find it informative, entertaining, inspirational and educational.

This book is dedicated to my precious little wonders. My children are my pride and joy. I look foward to the day when they each realize what an inspiration they have been in my life.

The life experiences of my children have inspired me so much, I have decided to embark on this exciting chapter of The Limit Is When You Say Stop™ for children and parents entitled PEJETALES©.

Sincerely,

Patrick Malcolm
Author/Motivational Speaker

INSIGHT

Peje, Alli, and Chrissy are brother and sisters. Each has decided to do their best to treat each other respectfully in hopes to treat everyone within their community with the same regard.

If each person takes the initiative to impact the life of every individual they meet positively, the lives of everyone will improve and the world would be a much better place to live in.

PEJETALES© is a collection of inspirational events told by Peje and his sisters Alli and Chrissy. We encourage every child to join Peje, Alli, and Chrissy during their experiences to see what it takes to overcome life's daily challenges and learn some of the values that are necessary in becoming a better *You*!

TABLE OF CONTENTS

Chapter One
Today Is A New Day... 02

Chapter Two
Forgiveness... 06

Chapter Three
Acceptance... 10

Chapter Four
Letting Go... 14

Chapter Five
Finding Inner Peace... 18

Chapter Six
You Are Not Your Mistakes.. 22

Chapter Seven
Agree to Disagree... 26

Chapter Eight
Distance Judging... 30

Chapter Nine
It's My Time.. 34

Chapter Ten
Our Relationship... 38

Chapter Eleven
A Word... 42

Chapter Twelve
Bullying.. 46

Chapter Thirteen
Thank You... 50

CHAPTER ONE

TODAY IS A NEW DAY

Peje, Alli and Chrissy's favorite thing to do in the morning, when they wake up, is to look out the window and watch the sun rise. *What is your favorite thing to do in the morning when you wake up? Today is a new day and a perfect time to thank God for another day.*

PEJETALES

ACTIVITY
Chapter 1 Word Find

Window has been found. Find the nine remaining words and write them on the line.

```
N E W Y D T I M E X F
K I C A B W P C C A H
W B T O G E T H E R M
O K O O L Q J O Y T O
D B F G O D R Y X C R
N W O K E I S A P C N
I U C M T K I D F P I
W V D E Q U X W T S N
S K N A H T Y L E Z G
```

1. **WINDOW**
2. NEW
3. MORNING
4. THANKS
5. GOD
6. TIME
7. LOOK
8. TOGETHER
9. JOY
10. DAY

3

THE LIMIT IS WHEN YOU SAY STOP ™

Today Is A New Day

Today: _ _ _ _ _ _ _ _ _ _ _ _ _ _
New: _ _ _ _ _ _ _ _ _ _ _ _
Day: _ _ _ _ _ _ _ _ _ _ _ _
Morning: _ _ _ _ _ _ _ _ _ _
Thanks: _ _ _ _ _ _ _ _ _ _
Time: _ _ _ _ _ _ _ _ _ _ _ _
God: _ _ _ _ _ _ _ _ _ _ _ _ _
Together: _ _ _ _ _ _ _ _ _
Joy: _ _ _ _ _ _ _ _ _ _ _ _
Window: _ _ _ _ _ _ _ _ _ _

Challenge: Write each word.

CHAPTER TWO

FORGIVENESS

During a game of crash derby, Peje accidentally broke Alli's toy. Alli was so hurt, she started to cry. Chrissy said, "C'mon Alli, don't cry. I don't think Peje meant to break your toy, right Peje?" "Right Chrissy," said Peje. Peje then apologized to Alli saying, "It was an accident Alli. I'm so sorry, please forgive me?" Alli replied, "It's okay Peje, I forgive you." *Why should we forgive others? Be quick to forgive and slow to anger. God forgives us, so we should forgive others.*

PEJETALES

ACTIVITY
Chapter 2 Connection

Connect the dots!

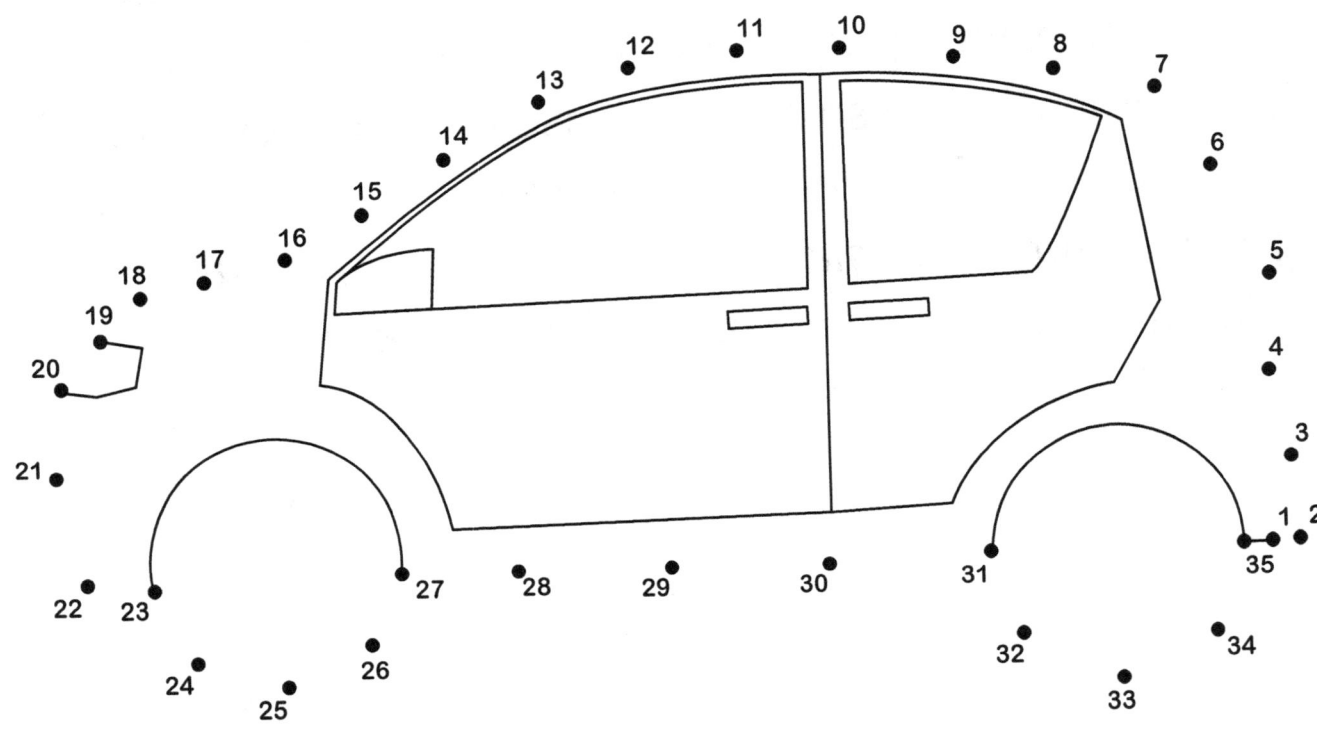

7

THE LIMIT IS WHEN YOU SAY STOP ™

Forgiveness

1   1   2

one one

3   4

5   6

7   8

9   10

Challenge: Write each number then spell each number.

CHAPTER THREE

ACCEPTANCE

While getting ready for school, the kids are looking in the mirror. They each take turns deciding what they like about themselves. Peje, he really likes his smile. Chrissy, she loves her eyelashses. Alli, she loves her curly hair. *What do you like about yourself? Regardless of what you find in the mirror, remember you are beautiful and wonderfully created by God.*

PEJETALES

ACTIVITY
Chapter 3 Face Facts

Match the seven areas of Chrissy's face.
Practice recognizing areas of your face. Write your first name below Chrissy's.

1. CHIN
2. EYES
3. NOSE
4. FOREHEAD
5. EARS
6. CHEEKS
7. MOUTH

Your First Name:

THE LIMIT IS WHEN YOU SAY STOP ™

Acceptance

Chin: ----------------
Ears: ----------------
Nose: ----------------
Eyes: ----------------
Forehead: ----------------
Cheeks: ----------------
Mouth: ----------------
Lips: ----------------
Eyebrows: ----------------

Challenge: Write each area of the face once.

CHAPTER FOUR

LETTING GO

Outside playing in the yard, Peje found his kite flew much better alone than when he held on. Peje's kite kept tugging to get away, so he let it go. "Fly kite, fly," Peje said, as he let go of his winder. "Wow! It worked," said Peje. Watching his kite fly through the air, with help from the wind, was so amazing. *Is there something you are holding on to that you feel you need to let go of? Sometimes, it is okay to let go. Letting go can open the door to happiness.*

PEJETALES

ACTIVITY
Chapter 4 Repeat After Me

Draw your answer in the boxes and spell it.

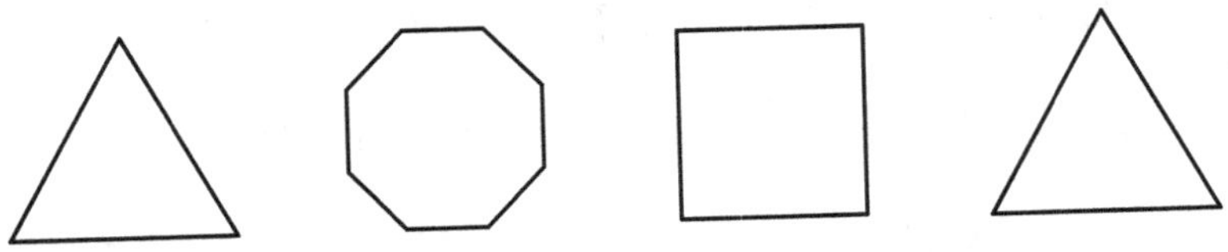

TRIANGLE   OCTAGON   SQUARE   TRIANGLE

NEXT SHAPE

RIGHT   DIAGONAL   UP   RIGHT

NEXT DIRECTION

4 5 6 4 5 6 4 5

NEXT NUMBER

THE LIMIT IS WHEN YOU SAY STOP ™

Letting Go

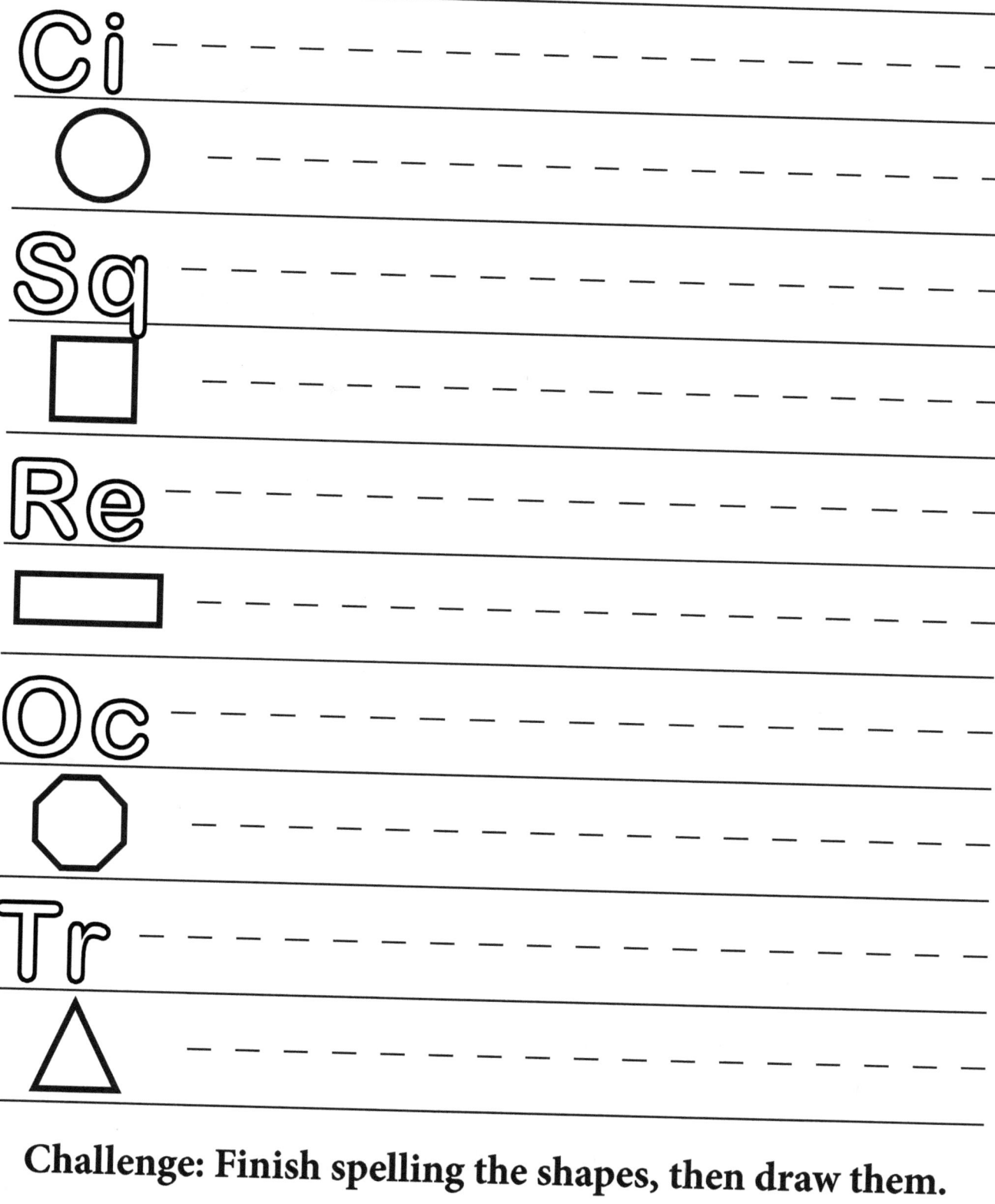

Challenge: Finish spelling the shapes, then draw them.

CHAPTER FIVE

FINDING INNER PEACE

Peje, Alli, and Chrissy enjoy telling each other stories because it brings each of them peace and joy. *What brings you peace and joy? Inner peace is not granted, it is created and only you can create your happiness.*

PEJETALES

ACTIVITY
Chapter 5 Count & Color

Identify each book and color them correctly.

☐ How many green books are there?

☐ How many books are on this shelf?

☐ How many yellow books are there?

☐ How many books are on this shelf?

☐ How many red books are there?

☐ How many books are on this shelf?

19

THE LIMIT IS WHEN YOU SAY STOP ™

Finding Inner Peace

Red: - - - - - - - - - - - - - - - - - - -
Orange: - - - - - - - - - - - - - - - -
Yellow: - - - - - - - - - - - - - - - -
Green: - - - - - - - - - - - - - - - -
Blue: - - - - - - - - - - - - - - - - -
Indigo: - - - - - - - - - - - - - - - -
Violet: - - - - - - - - - - - - - - - -
Black: - - - - - - - - - - - - - - - -
Rainbow: - - - - - - - - - - - - - - -

- -

Challenge: Color and write each word.

CHAPTER SIX

YOU ARE NOT YOUR MISTAKES

Peje was happy to share his cookies with Alli and Chrissy. Peje thought it would be great with some milk when, uh oh! He made a big spill and became very sad. Alli said, "Don't worry Peje, no one is perfect." "Yeah Peje, it's alright. We all make mistakes," said Chrissy. *Have you ever made a mistake? Accepting your mistakes while surrounding yourself with people who support and love you, will help you maintain the person you are and are trying to become.*

ACTIVITY
Chapter 6 Missing Vowels

The words below have missing vowels, can you guess the word?
Write the missing vowels.

1. M _ lk

2. Sh _ re

3. Sp _ ll

4. M _ st _ k _

5. C _ _ k _ _

6. S _ pp _ rt

a e i o u

THE LIMIT IS WHEN YOU SAY STOP ™

You Are Not Your Mistakes

a – – – – – – – – – – – – – –

e – – – – – – – – – – – – – –

i – – – – – – – – – – – – – –

o – – – – – – – – – – – – – –

u – – – – – – – – – – – – – –

Write a word with 1 vowel: – – – – – – – –

Write a word with 2 vowels: – – – – – – – –

Write a word with 3 vowels: – – – – – – – –

Write a word with 4 vowels: – – – – – – – –

– – – – – – – – – – – – – – – – –

Challenge: Write each vowel and think of words.

CHAPTER SEVEN

THE LIMIT IS WHEN YOU SAY STOP ™

AGREE TO DISAGREE

Peje, Alli and Chrissy heard a loud noise in the yard and each ran outside to see what happened, when they noticed their favorite tree toppled over. Alli said, "I think it was the wind." Chrissy said, "I think someone pushed it over." Peje replied, "Hmm. Well, there is no way to know what really happened to the tree, so let's agree to disagree." *Do you listen to both sides of the story when there is a disagreement? Sometimes our views will not be the same; always avoid being disrespectful during disagreements.*

PEJETALES

ACTIVITY
Chapter 7 Amazing Race

Give the maze below a try. Start from the center and find your way to the Finish. The limit is when you say stop™!

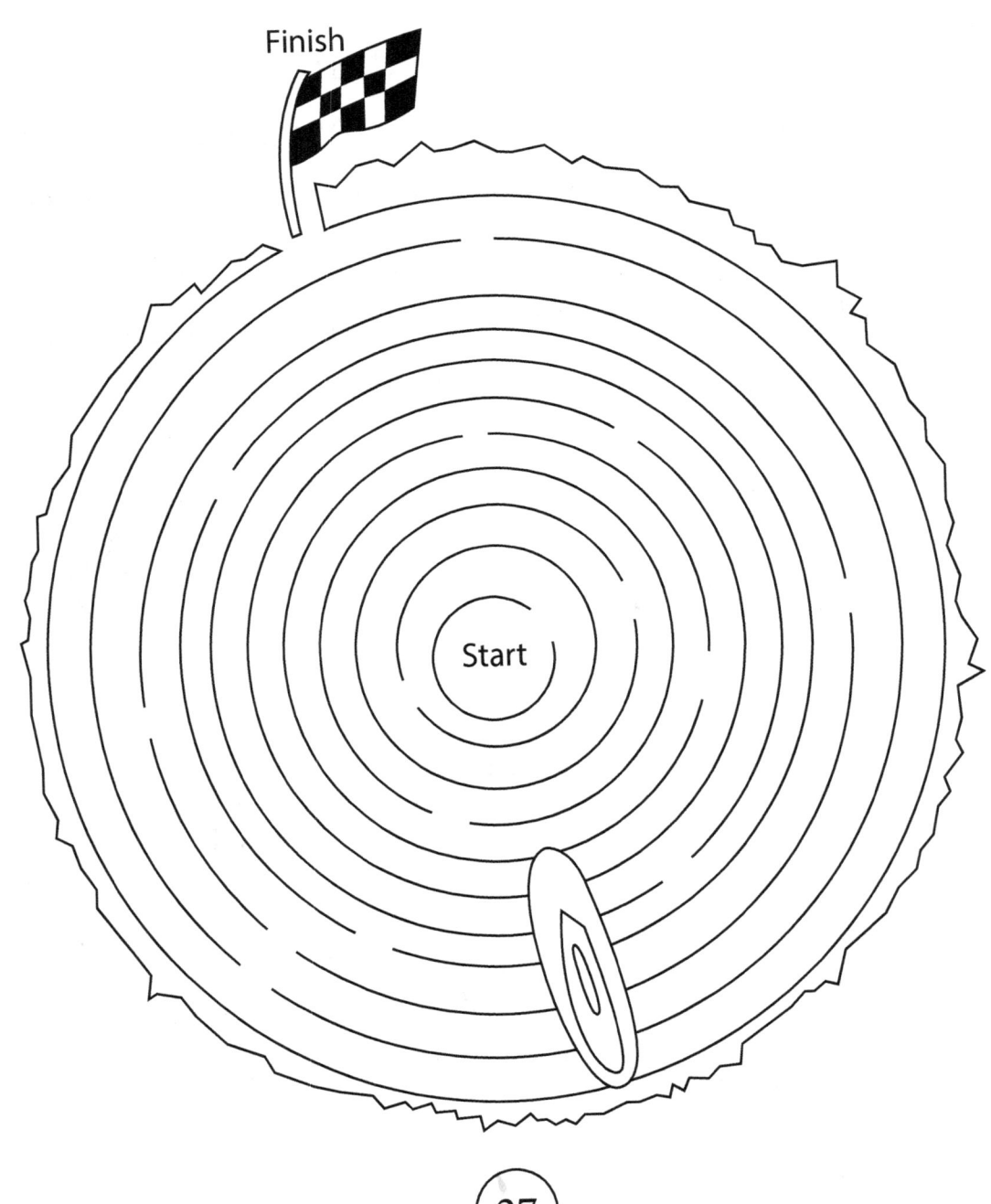

THE LIMIT IS WHEN YOU SAY STOP ™

Agree to Disagree

lisnte: listen

tlak: _____

arege: _____

disgreae: _____

avdio: _____

restepc: _____

thkin: _____

vewi: _____

tere: _____

Challenge: Solve the word jumbles in 3 minutes. Go!

CHAPTER EIGHT

DISTANCE JUDGING

Peje's favorite game to play is basketball. One day at the park, Peje asked a very tall boy sitting on the bench, "Would you like to play ball with me?" The boy replied, "I don't know how." Peje said, "You are so tall and you can't play ball?" The boy said, "I don't know, I guess I never tried." Peje replied, "It's okay, I can show you. You will never know you can't, unless you try." *Do you judge people you don't know? Instead of judging someone, take time to get to know them.*

PEJETALES

ACTIVITY
Chapter 8 Circle & Identify

Identify the number of balls below and color them as noted below.

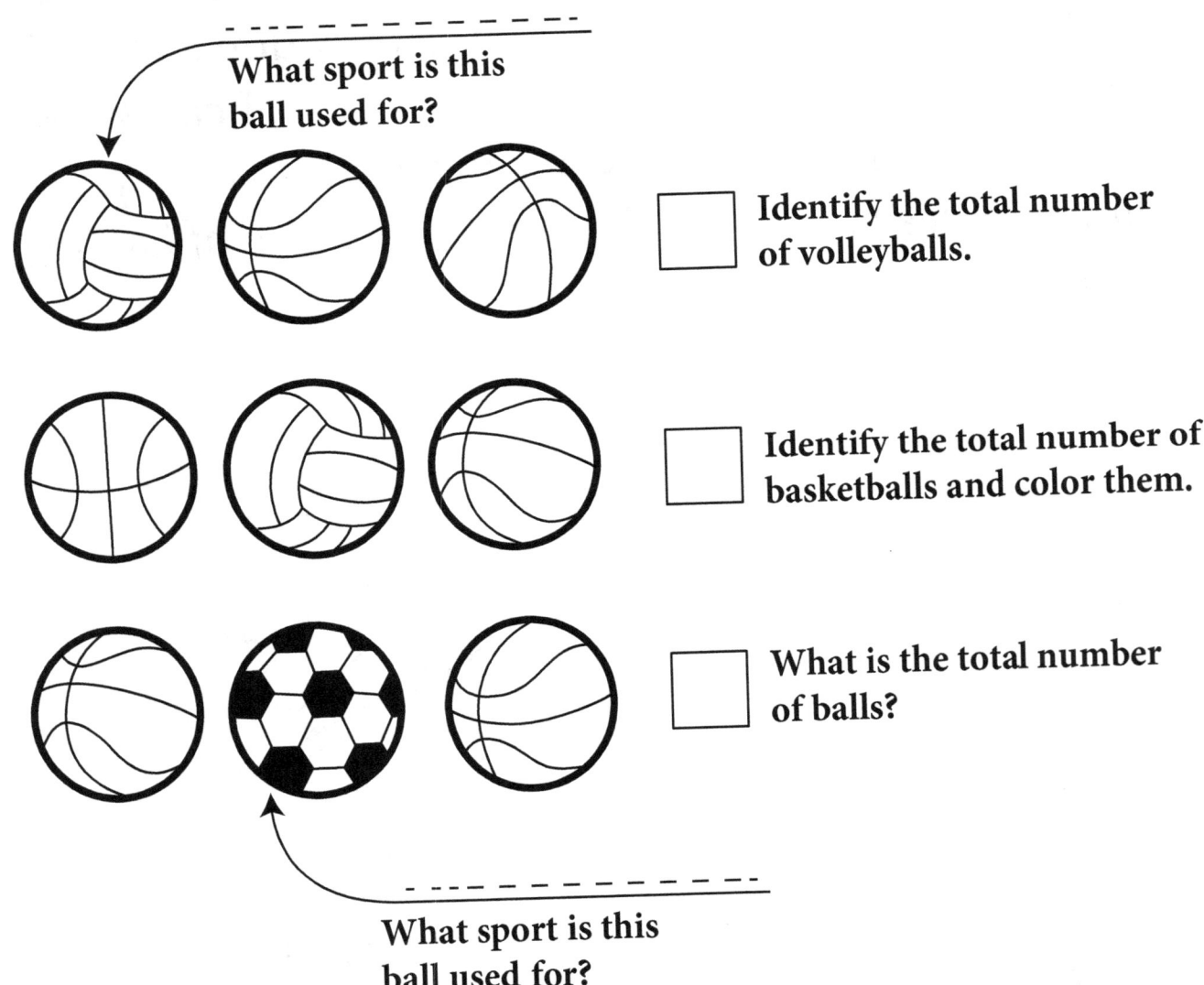

THE LIMIT IS WHEN YOU SAY STOP ™

Distance Judging

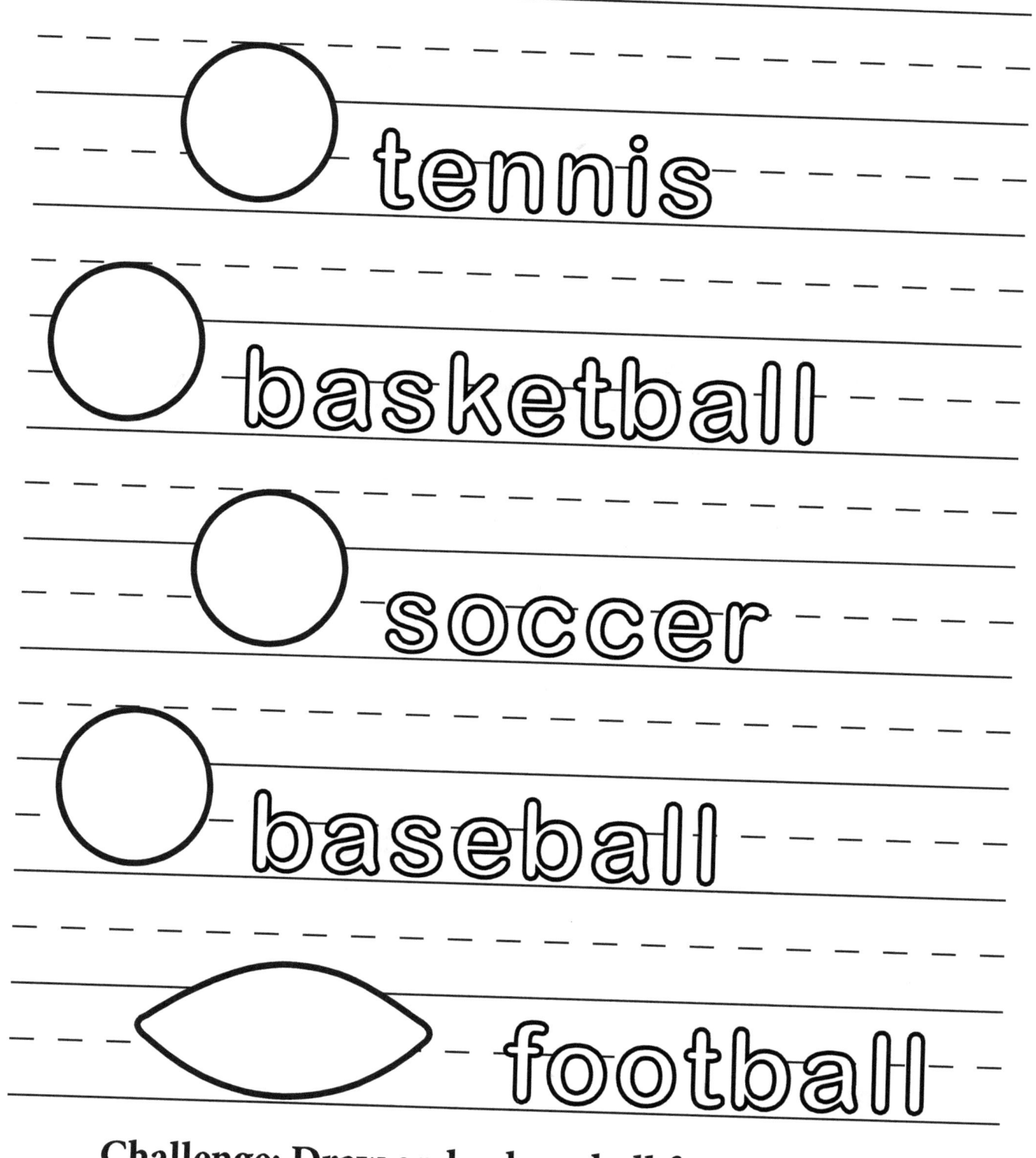

○ tennis

○ basketball

○ soccer

○ baseball

football

Challenge: Draw and color a ball from 5 sports.

CHAPTER NINE

IT'S MY TIME

When Peje is not with his sisters, Alli and Chrissy, he loves spending time playing with his cars and fixing them. *During your spare time, what do you like to do? No matter how much you get done, there will still be more to do. Learn to manage your time.*

PEJETALES

ACTIVITY
Chapter 9 Time After Time

Time is depicted in two ways below, digitally and analog. Write the time correctly and if you get stuck, know it is okay to ask for help.

8 : 10 eight : _ _ _	(clock showing ~8:10) eight : _ _ _
_ _ : _ _ twelve o'clock	(clock showing 12:00) _ _ _ _ _ _ _ o'clock
3 : 30 three : _ _ _ _ _ _	(clock showing 3:30) three : _ _ _ _ _ _

35

THE LIMIT IS WHEN YOU SAY STOP ™

It's My Time

Challenge: Arm and hand time; draw the time.

CHAPTER TEN

OUR RELATIONSHIP

Peje likes to go to the fair. While at the fair, his mommy reminds him to choose healthy foods and drinks, instead of candy and soda. *Why should we eat healthy foods? Before we can have a healthy relationship with others, we must have a healthy relationship with ourselves.*

PEJETALES

ACTIVITY
Chapter 10 Healthy Choices

Circle and color the healthy foods and beverages

| APPLE JUICE | CARROT | CHEESEBURGER | WATER |

| FRIES | BANANA | CANDY | SODA |

THE LIMIT IS WHEN YOU SAY STOP ™

Our Relationship

Water: _____

Tomatoe: _____

Carrot: _____

Orange: _____

Sandwich: _____

Cranberry: _____

Peanut: _____

Wheat: _____

Apple: _____

Pistachio: _____

Challenge: Write how many syllables are in each word.

CHAPTER ELEVEN

A WORD

Alli loves the monkey bars, but it's so hard. Every time she goes to grab the last bar she falls down. Defeated, Alli said, "Aww, I'll never be able to grab the bar." Chrissy said, "Don't say that Alli, just say you can do it." "That is true. If you keep saying "can't" Alli, you never will," replied Peje. *What words inspire you? Words are powerful; choose your words wisely and always believe in yourself.*

PEJETALES

ACTIVITY
Chapter 11 Positive vs Negative

Draw a line to match the positive word to the negative word.

POSITIVE  NEGATIVE

POSITIVE	NEGATIVE
CAN	MEAN
LOVE	LIE
KIND	BAD
TRUTH	CAN'T
GOOD	HATE

THE LIMIT IS WHEN YOU SAY STOP ™

A Word

Challenge: Write three sentences using a *positive* word and three sentences using a *negative* word.

CHAPTER TWELVE

BULLYING

During lunch time at school, Peje noticed a boy bullying another boy for his lunch. Peje quickly ran to tell a teacher. Moments later, Peje returned with the teacher. As soon as the teacher arrived, the bully was escorted to the principal's office and everyone applauded Peje's effort. *Have you ever been bullied? Bullying is wrong. If you see someone being bullied, don't be afraid to tell an adult as soon as possible.*

PEJETALES

ACTIVITY
Chapter 12 Safety First

Which objects are harmful? Circle and color the safe objects.

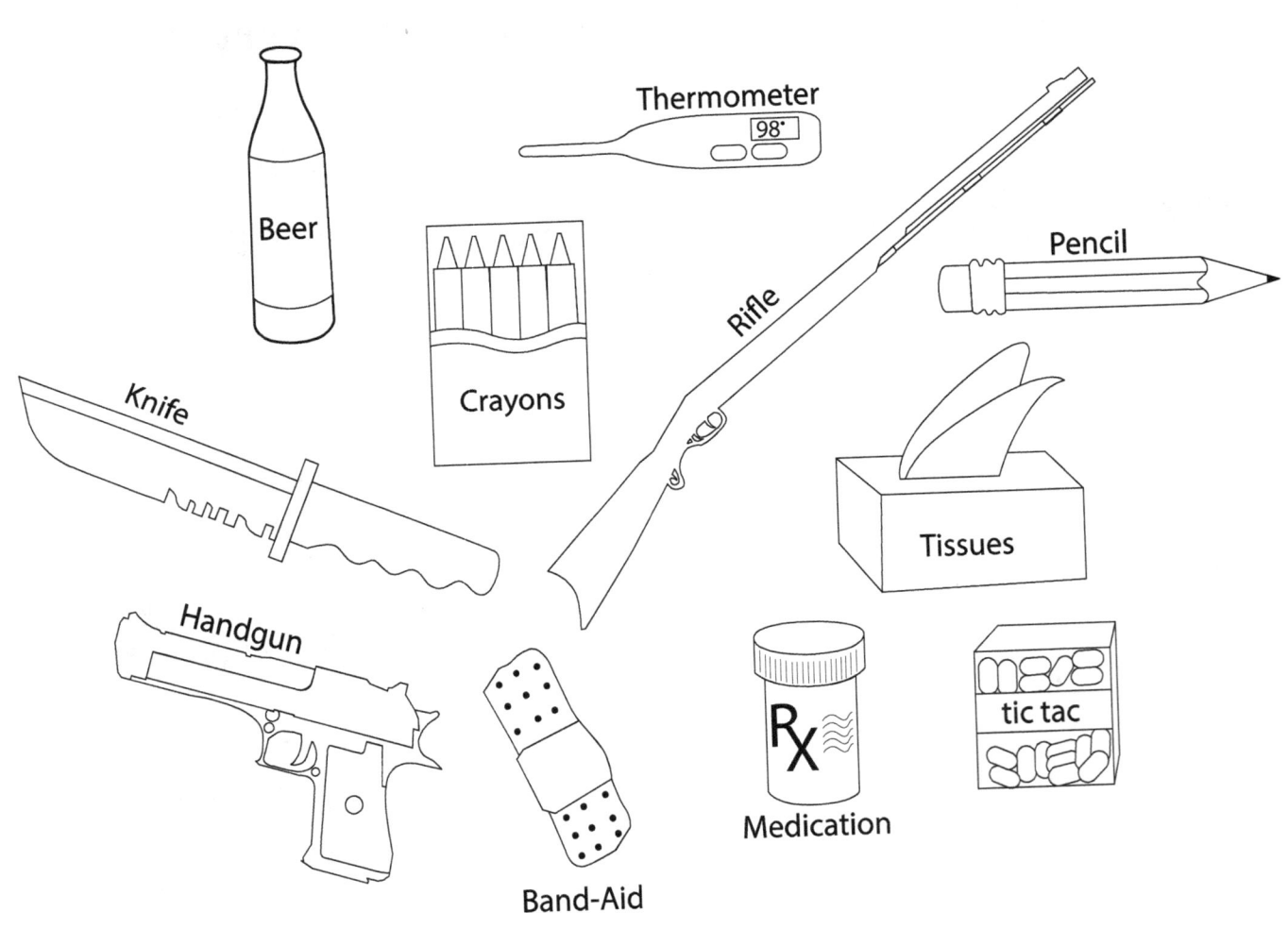

47

THE LIMIT IS WHEN YOU SAY STOP ™

Bullying

Challenge: Write three ways to prevent bullying.

CHAPTER THIRTEEN

THANK YOU

It's time to go to bed. Every night, Peje adds toothpaste to Alli and Chrissy's brushes. The girls are always so happy when he does and they always say, "Thank You Peje!" *Why should we always say, "Thank You?" If someone does a favor for you, it's best to be grateful and always remember to say, "Thank You."*

PEJETALES

ACTIVITY

Chapter 13 Thank You

**Trace each word below.
Thank you for reading PEJETALES©!**

THE LIMIT IS WHEN YOU SAY STOP ™

Thank You

Challenge: Write about what you are thankful for.

CONTACT US

If you love this book, do not hesitate to visit the following distributors below to show your support, provide feedback and share your review at:

AMAZON.com
AU-DE-CAN-US-UK
&
BARNES & NOBLE.com

Support via e-mail is welcomed at:
Pejepublishing@gmail.com

Also, do not hesitate to connect with us on:

   ❖   @pejepublishing

www.thelimitiswhenyousaystop.com